Short-Circuit
and betrayal
in child sexual abuse

A world without frontiers
Sharing experience and scientific opinions

Madeline Bosio

Rogerian Approach and Resilience

Copyright © 2012 Madeline Bosio

https://maddalenabosio.com/

Cover Design by Laura Nicli

iii

SHORT-CIRCUIT AND BETRAYAL IN CHILD SEXUAL ABUSE

Contents

Introduction

This work is by a Rogerian therapist seeking to overcome all sorts of scientific competition or criticism toward other psychological lines of thought, by sharing experiences and scientific opinions. It may be valuable in exploring more of the world of human behaviour and resilience.

The focus is on the area of human experience. The principle is to give clients a voice, providing material from direct clinical experience. Clinical relevance has validity for practitioners and experts in Naturalistic Research. The **key** for healing child sexual abuse lies in coming to terms with an uncompleted existential act "entangled" in the trauma.

The work is in line with a Rogerian approach and phenomenological point of view.

In my experience as a Person-Centred therapist, an expert in sex therapy and working on an experiential level, I have had the opportunity to meet people with sexual or behavioural disorders, victims of sexual abuse in childhood. My intent, in this paper is to reveal the knots and entanglements caused by the traumatic sexual abuse experience.

The work involves the person's history as a whole. Material regarding sexual abuse emerges during a classic psychotherapy so sexual abuse is an integral part of the therapeutic process. Even though sex abuse is an experience that sometimes occurs "outside" the regular stream of life, it becomes interwoven with the victim's life and affects certain interactions.

My intention is to **reveal the main aspects concerning abuse and the therapeutic process, restoring resilience and thus "the actualizing tendency".** (Rogers) Healing of the Self.

I shall explore wounded regions that hold the experience of abuse, the uncompleted existential act and a specific aspect, which is the key to reiteration.

My deep gratitude goes to the neuroscientists, in particular to doctor Peter A. Levine and to doctor Stephen W. Porges who provide evidence, on a neurophysiological level, of what I am explaining on an experiential and psychological level from a phenomenological point of view. In other words what I say also "makes sense" from a neurological point of view.

I have read numerous books written by famous neurology experts. There are expositions regarding phenomenology by famous names in philosophy, in phenomenology, in psychology and their contribution to the understanding of behavioural patterns from a neurological point of view, but I have never found a word about Carl Roger's contribution to their research. In my opinion, Carl Roger's work and research have not been accorded the dignity they deserve. I hope that this work will provide evidence of the success of Person- Centred therapy and honour Roger's theory and the philosophical "way of being".

Non-directive therapy relies on the importance of establishing respect and trust in the relationship between therapist and client. Therapy moves along the pathway indicated by the client's frame of reference to which the therapist gives positive and unconditional regard. The paradigm used is the client's frame of reference.

The basis of the Rogerian approach is in tune with concepts and principles pertaining to Existential philosophy, so it differs from the structural theories underpinning the Freudian line of thought and from Behavioural theories, which are in tune with Positivist philosophy. The phenomenal world unfolds within "individuality". Though different, in every individual there are those universal values that I call Cosmic Values, and that inevitably hold us all in a symphony of Respect and Love.

Rogerian research operates in the field of "natural science". Rogers drew attention to attitudes, thus highlighting "meaning" rather than techniques. Neuroscience has scientifically proved that all behaviours are an outcome of feelings and emotions. Self -consciousness is an authentic "dwelling" with the Essence of oneself. It is an internal instrument anchored firmly to everyday life.

Chapter 1 – Sex abuse and trauma

Before starting my analysis, I need to point out certain main aspects underlying the Person-Centred Approach.

It is widely known that our "unsatisfied needs" in childhood become the main "targets" of an endless research in the attempt to attain what we were supposed to receive from our caregivers (Maslow and Rogers). Experiences of sexual abuse, besides causing a trauma, are in some cases, burdened with this specific aspect of life. This means that the experience of sexual abuse interweaves with the victim's life and "way of being". As we know, sexual abuse is an experience included in the so-called "traumatic experiences", which have the taste of a "deadly trap", both for the victim as well as for the abuser.

Should we imagine a victim's cry, it would be:

"I beg you, help me heal my wounds"…

Should we imagine an abuser's cry, it would be:

"I beg you, lead me out from worlds that art not mine"…

The experience suffered by these victims will influence their lives with two kinds of behaviours.

In one case, the behaviour is of a person who "remains a victim":

*It is a reiteration of the experience of being the "victim".

*It is a crystallized experience.

*On an emotional level, it preserves something of the "suffered"… "Emotions keep on calling".

In another case, it is a "repeating with others" of the "denied" experience.

*It is "not me"

*On the emotional level, everything "is silenced"… "The world of feelings is a haunted place…"

Both experiences cause a "short circuit". This is the aspect I shall examine.

Let us start from the beginning of this dramatic experience, moving through the tunnel from darkness and chains, and reaching the light again… a long journey…

Sexual abuse begins with an overwhelming incapability to experience the "here and now", in other words, "the event". This gives rise to surrender, the child paralyzed with fear followed by "shut down", with all the consequences described later.

That is not all. The event "stops or "interrupts" the existential act "in being" before the molesting act: "interaction betrayed". Thus, we have to deal with two acts/experiences of life: trauma and the uncompleted existential act. This is the point where the "film" of the stream of life is jammed, giving way to a short circuit.

It is a short circuit springing from the betrayed existential act that "triggers" the reiteration of sexual experience. An area of the brain triggers the symbolized process.

I agree with Peter A. Levine when he states that the "psyche, or brain, can shut down but EYES DON'T FORGET"… and the trouble is that they keep on "looking into the world", with eyes of INNOCENCE…

The statement is widely confirmed by my clients.

The experience

Let us now go back to the moment when the experience is taking place:

We have seen that the experience of "staying", that is, experiencing the event in its "here and now", is "impossible".

Defence mechanisms of the event do not work: "flight –attack" like running away or screaming. It is a no way out attack (Levine).

A client during a session:

"In the "here and now" time is dilated: one is a "whole" made up of many components, whereas "in fright" time is "contracted": it stops; you are a "micron".

As I have just said, and the client confirms this principle, one is incapable "of staying" with the event underway, I mean "staying in the experience".

A first moment of astonishment, followed by paralyzing terror - an overwhelming helplessness - the feeling of a "missing protector" - thus, being at the mercy of the Self… hence a deadly fear. The shut - down: the trauma.

The child is facing something beyond any

capability and does not even understand what is going on. Moreover, it is something that has nothing to do with what the expectations and promises were. Something "outside the child's frame of reference". Sometimes (depending on the age) it involves a sphere (sexual feelings) that has nothing to do with the child's developmental stage.

The sequence of feelings experienced, are usually the following:

1 - Astonishment, but also fear:

* No proper instruments for any sort of reaction (screaming, running away, fighting, saying no and so on)

*No proper constructions for such a "reality"

* Without personal power to oppose the abuser's power

* A feeling of helplessness and loneliness. Feelings of being lost, hopeless, perplexed, confused. The mind does not work. Emotions are overwhelming. The child is puzzled and bewildered. The "I-Me" (subjectivity of the being: Boncinelli) is under extreme strain. The "I-Me" is fallacious.

A survival instinct senses the need for a presence (a caregiver) … a need for protection. …"Where were you?" This is what victims usually say, because there is the "human need" to escape from the "feeling of uneasiness"… out of a situation not determined by her/himself.

2 - At that moment, the child senses the "absence" of a "presence" and this brings the "experience" of a "deep void", which opens up from the primal need for protection, but cannot be satisfied. It is a need

that turns into paralyzing terror and helplessness, a "deranged experience", with no rescue by a caregiver.

3 - The paralyzing fear is managed by getting into a sort of "stand by" situation ...waiting for "the thing" to come to end. Sometimes there are also sexual feelings, depending on the age. There is a chaotic stream of emotions...

"The thing" is made up of different sorts of feelings and emotions.

4 - Should this "way of being" fail, another way out is a "split" or a psychic dissociation.

5 - Whatever the situation, it is clear that there is a fragmentation of the self. The personality will split into disunited parts.

6 - As explained before, there could be a "way out" that is: "experiencing the here and now". It is an experience that goes "beyond" the child's "existing" in the world.

The paralyzing experience, "external" to the child's day-to-day life, could be seen as a "Black Hole" THAT TAKES IN WHATEVER PASSES BY... "WHY?"...

Before the "offensive act", there was a different "phenomenal reality" going on: the child's reality of that moment had nothing to do with the offence. The abuser too was pretending something else....

Before being "cheated", as regards the interaction with the offender, the child was expecting to "experience something else".

This means that the abuse contains two realities, at that same moment. One is the child's reality. The second reality is unexpected… a new and unknown one.

It is "an unexpected event" and determines an uncompleted existential act. An uncompleted act consists of what the child believed "was supposed to be", since a child too has its own line of thought .The child had an expectation…

I am referring to the child's frame of reference containing a personal history that inevitably affects all relationship (R.D. Laing – S.W. Porges). We are talking about the existential world and values with which individuals interact in the world.

Thus, the child's experience is impaired on two levels:

* The first is a distortion of the personal inner being of the child's world.

* The second belongs to the external event.

In my opinion, it is the betrayed expectation that opens the black hole: the uncompleted existential act that "takes in" the negative experience (like a wounded monster). (quantic physics confirms it: two different frequencies that determine an implosion).The consequence is that every time the victim comes in touch/relationship with a person who has certain features, the black hole unavoidably "attracts" (stimulates) the victim's attention, thus a reiteration of the abuse. In other words, the uncompleted existential act triggers the reiteration of the abusive experience.

The betrayed expectation, which contains a need, causes the "short-circuit". Neuroscience confirms that all behaviours have to do with emotions and feelings.

First example:

EXPECTATION	PROMISE
Oh! How beautiful!	Take you to the
Very caring with me	Movies
Friendly;	
Takes an interest in me…	

** He is taking me to the movies (The promise)
** He fulfils my "need" for
attention and lovingness… (The dream)

B U T

*The promise betrayed.	The promise changed
*An unexpected experience	
is suffered	* Abuse

Second Example:

Oh! How beautiful.	Come and play with my puppy
Someone to soothe my loneliness	

B U T

*The promise is betrayed	* The promise is changed
*An unexpected experience	
is suffered	* Abuse

We can sum this up as follows:

1- Trauma is a "specific" paralyzing event along the stream of life.

2- The stream of life is "disrupted" by an uncompleted existential act.

3- A short-circuit will trigger a reiteration in behavioural patterns.

4- Neuroscience confirms all behaviours relate to feelings and emotions.

Chapter 2 - The Therapeutic Process

Psychotherapy consists of repairing pieces of a shattered structure. It heals wounds and *singles out a fragment* that does not belong to the victim.

Play Therapy with children, gives positive outcomes and the work differs from what I am describing. My work is with adults.

Recovery goes through two stages:

- One stage concerns the abuse in itself. The victim will go through the emotions and feelings experienced when abused.

- The other stage concerns the defeated expectations and the uncompleted existential act that cause a short circuit.

Some of these feelings and emotions are at a conscious level. Others surface along the path within the therapeutic process. (M. Bosio)

The main feelings experienced: being betrayed

– being defeated – having "lost the game" (game of life) – being without protection (caregiver) – being alone – being helpless – being at the mercy of the world – being hopeless – a deadly fear – sometimes terror. Recognizing physical violence and revisiting, if necessary, erotic feelings.

These experiential feelings will be integrated with the traumatic experience. They will be given the right to citizenship, in order to restore a healthy actualizing tendency. There is a recovery of personal power.

The key lies in **accepting** reality, **accepting** defeat, **accepting** one has lost the game, **accepting** it was "me" experiencing the event. I was "in" the event. Sometimes there is a "split".

Along with the unfolding of all these aspects, in its crude taste, new healing elements appear to reinforce the victim's personality. Feelings of warmth and tenderness towards oneself move in.

The main new feelings are the following:

Being a survivor – I came out "alive" from those emotional storms – I've been in a place where not even angels dare to go – I lost the game - no more "ifs" or "buts" (that is blaming myself) – the experience was lived and felt on my skin in the first person – besides being a victim I was also a protagonist.

This last aspect is very important to understand. The victim is at the same time the **protagonist**. That means I am a victim as regards my offender, but at the same time I am also the one who "experienced" the "event"… deep in my soul and body.

As far as I only see the victim in me, (I-thou) I cannot see the protagonist (I-me).This aspect is explained below.

There will be feelings of shame and guilt… But they will give way to a restored innocence.

The outcome is:
- I am special because I am a survivor
- I am a hero because
  °I came out of that hell on my own
  °even heroes can lose the game. Even losing a game, a hero is always a hero.
- It is a rescued experience… LILIES GROW OUT OF MUD…

The part presented so far is the re-elaboration of the "external" event.

According to my experience, healing is possible only when the "pattern" triggering reiteration is, first singled out, and then solved. It is a re-elaboration of an "inner part" involved in the event.

Let us go back to the short-circuit: in my experience, I have noticed that an **area of the brain triggers a symbolized process**. This aspect is the exposal of this work.

So far, we have healed the wounds of the sexual experience: the "traumatic" event. The "I-Thou".

Now let's look at "unfolding" the anomalous behaviour set up when the flow of existential experience was interrupted: the "I –me".

I will divide this into two parts in order to make the explanation as simple as possible. The therapeutic process is complex and advances as the client emerges. This is a peculiarity of the Person- Centred approach.

The uncompleted existential act

As we know from existential philosophy, an **existential act** behaves according to feelings, cravings, expectations, hopes, dreams, need, fears that lead us to make choices and thus *"perform" an experience*. Neuroscience confirms that behaviours come from feelings and emotions.

In other words, **every existential act is a choice**.

Going back to the victim and the abuser, the interaction/event guided by the offender, turns out to be far away from the victim's frame of reference, in the "here and now". The child is *experiencing something that differs totally from expectations and feelings.*

We must bear in mind that children *look into the world with "eyes of innocence"* and from a developmental frame of reference, this is the age of innocence.

The act suffered is so far from the victim's thoughts that astonishment, followed by confusion, fear and all sorts of feelings, come up in those first moments in the child's phenomenal world.

From here on comes the train of feelings and emotions already described.

We can see that at one "end" of disruption into the stream of life is **"expectation"**… and on the other end the beginning of an **unexpected** and incomprehensible **"storm"**… These two ends cannot match, because of their different meanings. What's more, one of the existential acts does not take place.

Hence, we have the following:

The child's existential choice… *expectation…* abuse… *betrayal* by the offender… interruption of the experience… trauma and "being in disruption".

This is where the beginning and end of the victim's existential act will not join in order to continue the string of life in progress, but triggers the reiteration of the sexual experience. Why? **Some of the future interactions will flow (are attracted) through the "break" of the uncompleted act. Biology and physics can explain this aspect.**

Often the child will pick up certain types of "acting out" such as sexualized behaviours, that are a cry to the world, but are sometimes misunderstood by adults.

Only psychotherapy can stop the triggering phenomenon, tracing the story back to its original frame of reference, owing to the existential rule that states:

"Each existential act has an intentionality – an actualization – thus a historicity".

Neuroscience confirms the rule. (Levine)

The point is that traumatic experience causes a "break" in the here and now of the child's reality that is contextualized in a world of "innocence". "Children look into the world with eyes of innocence…" Their eyes of innocence become frozen at this stage.

This is an important aspect to consider because individuals, who have been through the experience of abuse, keep on reading reality with the eyes of innocence. Even when an adult builds the defensive behaviour of a suspicious person, in certain circumstances, that person will fall into a trap by using the "eyes of innocence".

Following is a spotlight on "landmarks" in order to understand why "eyes of innocence.

We know that feelings experienced during the early years of life become the "essence" of our "being".

It is during this developmental stage that we build our future "landmarks" (Reference points). In our early days of life, there are no landmarks. The child is in symbiosis with the caregiver and depends entirely on "the outside world". Nevertheless, *defence mechanisms are* helping us. The defensive system is *physiological*: I am hungry… I cry… I get desperate… I go into a storm of emotions… If somebody comes and satisfies my hunger, I happily fall asleep. If nobody comes, I get into a sort of *anaclitic depression* and **fall asleep**; this is what happens in orphan-asylums.

It is only later that a *psychological* system starts building up. In the experience of abuse, a child has no defences. Reality (sexual event) is beyond the child's capacity: the child is incapable of understanding. Anguish, sorrow, wounds, pain, dismay, fear are beyond their "coping" power. There is a stormy stream of emotions. Only a caregiver has the power (duty) to act as a border for the flow of emotions. This would enhance a containment (avoid a flood) of feelings that could be shared- recognized – confirmed – accepted, with the aid of the adult.

Why does this occur?

The answer is very simple: the child's landmarks are still "external" to the self. The caregiver is he who helps the child to "internalize" experience. When this does not happen, the child will be at the mercy of the "wild world". The child is still looking into the world with eyes of innocence, thus confused and scared. A client explained: "*being in a mixer*". Fear has a deadly taste, and the self is unable to protect itself. At that age, owing to what is going on, the child is experiencing something beyond reality, capacity, intelligence, reactivity. No safety of the self. The failure is total.

Pillars of life

Now let us have the vision of the *"Pillars of Life"* involved in this game of life and from which, all that the two protagonists experience, spreads out.

There are two Pillars:

> The offender's pillar... of power
> The victim's pillar... of existence

In the light of this vision, the offender is an abuser of power. The victim undergoes **the expropriation of "being"**. Destruction goes beyond the frontier of dignity and human respect. It crosses the "living space" (gestalt) beyond which "not even angels dare to tread"... there, **the existing is shattered**... *"There, there is my heart my soul, my roots"*, says a client.

Here dwells **"being in destruction"** for the self (I-me), and **"being defeated"**, as to the other (I –Thou).

Existing breaks into pieces ("fragments" says a client) with consequences of different degrees of severity. On an "existential" level, the prices to pay and to face are high. The event has such a level of destruction because there is a break in the harmony of the Self, caused by several disruptions having the taste of death.

This **death** comes from the **"essence"** of the child's life. It is the pain and existential fear of **"being"** without a protection. It leads to feelings of being helpless, incapable of coping with the "unknown"... the "being" is at the mercy of nothingness… hopeless… thus terrorized… The **surrender** of the "being," and then "existing" **crumbles.**

Cl …*In that moment,* **time** *exists no more…*
Th …*Yes… there is a black hole…*
Cl *That's what I am feeling now…*

On a psycho-neurological level I believe there is a difference between a trauma experienced by a person or an animal… It's fear that surrenders to the violence of the offender, the same as in animals, but for the human being there **is confusion and "the unknown"** and it's the unknown that crushes the child's "sense of existing". Even though young, there is "consciousness of being". These are the words of adults abused in childhood.

The outcome is a *deadly wound* within the structure of **existing in the world**.

The victim in childhood, who is the adult today, encounters those experiential pieces of the past. As an adult, they are no longer in need of "defensive banks", but nevertheless need to rely on warm, empathic holding by a psychotherapist, to let go and allow themselves to enter and experience the **trauma**, the flow of all kinds of emotions and feelings once banished or frozen and somehow contained by defence systems set up at that time. In spite of all defensive attempts, they have jammed the flowing tide of existence… and caused a history of reiterations of abuse. Animals have no denied emotions.

Along the experiential process, the client will go back to these wounded parts of the self to let feelings and emotions flow, give life to those "frozen" and sometimes denied experiences that shackle the flow of existing…

We can now move on with a few examples.
First example. **Mandy**
Here are fragments of therapy sessions.
Mandy is a client who has gone a long way in her psychotherapy. We shall "meet" her, again further on.
Cl …*When I have to do something new, I already organize a way out…*
Th …*Do you have an example?*
Cl *When I work on a project* (in social work) *I make sure, everything is perfect… I am calm, confident. Then* **something blocks** *me and I get someone else to introduce and carry out my work…* (For disabled adults).
Th *You decide to let go… sort of giving up…*
Cl: *Yes…*
Th. *Here, in this case, it's possible to do so … maybe in other things you can't do this…*
Cl. *Yes! For example on a highway or having to stop along a road…*
Th. *Behind the stage you are strong… you are safe…* (I am reflecting a confrontation between two different situations: a stage – a highway).
Cl. *Yes, yes…*
Th. *Behind the stage you have control over things…*
Cl. *Yes…*
Th. *On the highway it's the highway controlling you…*
Cl. …(A long silence….)… (Few minutes)…
Th. *Where are your feelings?* (She had changed breathing and countenance)
Cl. *Fear…* (Silence…) *I felt a pang… a splash… fear…* (Cry)…
Th. (feedback her contents) *There lies all your*

"helplessness". You feel you cannot use your power or control the situation on a highway or the audience in a congress... (I am in empathy with her and mirroring her contents...)

Cl. *This is what I used to feel with John* (her childhood abuser) ...

Th. *You couldn't do anything else...*

Cl. *I was there helpless ... impotent... I could only stay...* (Cries)...

Th. *You were there alone... on your own... forsaken... neglected... a child disappears.* (I say so because it is this moment that gives rise to the feeling of being alone, in a reality bigger than the child's phenomenal world). Here is the sense of having to give up: **"I could only stay,"** she said. Surrender, being defeated... I am her mirror in this moment... confronting her with her past. The feelings experienced in the "dramatic event". In other sessions, she had **voiced** these feelings

Cl. *...Yes...* (Silence...) *nevertheless, I remain myself...*

At last! After tackling these moments many times, she has come out! Survived - came out alone— through her feelings ... At last the client is able to say this: she comes out alive - she survived all this ... at this point, her reality is changing. It is a healing of her inner relationship. **(I -me).** I must point out that, before reaching **this step**, she previously had to go through several stages: experiencing her being betrayed and defeated, (*This has to do with the unfinished existential act*)... She lost the game... a reality she cannot change...

I "resume" using "her" pieces of the puzzle that came out from other sessions and say:

Th. *Yes...if you accept being defeated... lost the game...*

like a phoenix… you rise again… you remain… (A metaphor backing up what she is saying, consumed by her own act: loss and dying and rise to freshness and life from her own ashes…

Cl. He won… he already has his WAYS TO ESCAPE… *don't speak… we have a secret* and so on (She is talking in the present, because has gone back to that moment and is re-experiencing the scene…)

Th. *Yes, this is the reality of "that moment"…*

Cl. *I remember that last week I was in Rimini, at the seaside with Robby* (her husband). *I remember* (goes back to those days) *the beach where I used to go when a little girl…where John used to work in the summer season… I saw the beach again and then him, and I see myself going towards him… and I embrace him…* (Silence… silence)

Th. *Maybe something drove you to do so?*

Cl. …(cries)… *inside myself I said to him: "You couldn't do otherwise…* (keeps crying… a deep sigh…)

Here takes place the **"humanization"** of the being. Just beyond this line appears the "absolute" where the TWO ENDS (the opposites) meet and the meeting wells up in respect and compassion. They nullify, harmony restored… **"This is how it went"…** there is no blaming… no right or wrong… no forgiving…but only: ***"THIS IS"…*** because the only truth: **reality.** Reality bears no judicial value: It "just is". This is the reason why I state that if I say "I forgive you" it means I am still in the "being" of judging, so I still am in two realities: what is and what should have been.

We can find a similar statement in quantic theory: *"there is a thing and the opposite; energy can materialize and de-materialize…"*

This experiencing is a transcending from an

existential way of being to a sort of cosmic love or way of feeling. It is the opposite of emptiness... here, Mandy's "being," is of compassion.

We are also in line with existential philosophy: transcending the "drama of being" and its "narrow" values. Embracing "universal" values: respect – acceptance – responsibility – love – compassion.

We can say that *an existential act* is a **pure act of consciousness** and **its** *pillar* is **respect.**

Here everything has made a shift toward the ABSOLUTE. Transcending the being, there is the absolute. The border that marks the "limit," the end, opens on to the "infinite".

"When you transcend the world of matter
You enter a spiritual dimension
Where "I-Thou" "This and That"
Become unity with the Whole"
The Tao of Physics. (Capra)

On a therapeutic level, we can see that some interventions by the therapist in empathy with the client's experiencing provide the way to explore and connect with deep hidden feelings and emotions.

I must point out that Mandy reached this stage of healing because she had already dealt with the "betrayed expectation: the unfinished existential act" (I-Me) in the promise. We shall see this further on.

Feelings and humanization

Let us go back to Mandy. When she says: *"You couldn't do otherwise"* she changed her feelings of winners and losers, transcending the being.

Humanizing the being-in- the world in itself and the next step is the "absolute". That is **"going beyond ones being"**… and being free…

In this case, when Mandy tunes into universal values, like respect and compassion, the "I" and the "Thou" become a whole with the cosmic. This can take place only when the "I-Me" experience is restored: the *sexualisation* of the *"event"*. (M. Bosio)

Martin Buber and Carl Rogers say: *Accepting reality, the* **"limits"** *this specific reality calls for, and that is "being defeated", Mandy gives rise to a sense of* **"relativity"**: *a "limit" But a limit is actually the border to the sense of* **"infinity"**.

THUS, "my limit" becomes for me "my" infinite… THUS: I am free…

I repeat that the reiteration of abuse ends only after dealing with the un-completed existential act. The key is in the Short-Circuit.

From a clinical point of view, what did the psychotherapist offer in this long voyage?

It is not easy to explain! Maybe not even possible on technical and theoretical levels, when the process runs along the lines of relating to a phenomenal world.

Nevertheless, we can point out some aspects.

Containment:

A warm presence to "lean" on. It consists of being an understanding and empathic container in difficult and highly emotional moments. This is the "holding" a caregiver should give to a child.

Empathy:

Recognizing and sharing emotions (intellectualizations, hallucinations or other) at the client's rhythm and level. This is important for understanding the dynamics that lead to painful wounds hidden in the darkness of the client's being.

Focusing:

Consists of focusing on feelings that are on the edge of awareness, in order to go deeper into the world of emotions and feelings relating to particular aspects of the client's story. It is a focusing and reflecting, deepening and expanding.

Metaphors:

Developing congruent symbols for the organismic experiencing .The therapist singles out words, images or metaphors, body expressions, fitting the "implicitly felt". (Rogerian "felt meaning").

Mirroring:

The therapist is in the position to interact with the client and at the same time be "in congruency" with the **"outside reality"**. Bringing out and empathizing aspects or feelings of the **"inside world"**, on the "brink" of expression…that is "catching" a feeling or a way of being in "that" moment and "in that" place, not letting it slip away, thus making it explicit for the client.

Metaphorically, I could say we are in perfect empathy with the client. "There", in "that specific" moment where the client has **the wound** and the therapist the **"actualizing"** ingredient.

Acceptance:

Roger's Unconditional Positive Regard. This means giving dignity and respect to "exsisting" and "being" whatever it may be. It means keeping in touch with the client's "frame of reference".

This aspect is in tune with principles of existential philosophy.

Reading Reality:

This concerns the reality of the client's story. That is, adjusting the past reality according to a healthy actualizing development during the child's growth, and compared to "what" really happened in the client's childhood. What "should have been" and what really happened. It is an "immersion" in reality.

There is no doubt that behind all this experiencing, there must be also clinical and theoretical knowledge as regards sex and abuse. (M. Bosio)

Respect:

It is love without judgement... *"Universal values are nothing but an act of pure consciousness..."*

Humanization of the Experiences:

This comes out on its own...

Once more I owe thanks to prof. Peter L Levine and to prof. S.W. Porges, who explained the "ways of being" using neuroscience, hence giving scientific value to Roger's work. Phenomenology, psychology, physics, biology, neurology have something in common.

The star
The anemone
The schizophrenic
The medusa
Have something in common
And we with them
Gregory Bateson

That the "that" and the "this"
cease to be opposites in the
very essence if the Tao

Capra

Chapter 3 – Reiteration

Now there is still another piece of Mandy's story to examine. It regards her "uncompleted" existential act concerning the "I–Me" that triggers **reiteration.**

It has to do with "strings" that go down into her story as a child.

Here I agree with Porges who says that certain traumatic events need psychotherapy in spite of solving the trauma with exercises or behavioural interventions. In fact, sometimes, even though the traumatic event is over, and the person goes back to certain environmental conditions or ways of being, or specific interactions, the same pattern will turn up. There is the risk of "reiterating" the same experience because "emotions" do not respond to the "intellect". It is the "short circuit," that triggers reiteration. Change can take place "only" through the "experience of mourning" and coming to terms with certain aspects of "reality".

What's the difference?

Neuroscience relies on "what happened".

Research is carried out on "something" that happened.

Phenomenology relies on the "meaning" of the experience. On the description of the story; on thoughts and feelings.

The former is a description from the "outside", the latter a description from the "inside".

As regards Mandy, she *had an account to settle* with **a need/dream**, entangled in the uncompleted existential act. We shall see this further.

Second example: The Trap

June does not know why "it" happens. She says that just about every evening, after dinner she wants to go to the coffee shop not far from home...

Cl. ...*When I enter, I catch sight of a guy* (so "she" chooses)... *and I go towards him, because at once I automatically feel the desire to "fuck" him...*

Th. ...*If automatic, it must be very strong...*

Cl. ...*There is a sort of a need for revenge... Once I've had sex, I feel restored... I say to myself Ha! There you are! I cheated you! But the day after it starts all over again...*

In childhood, June was "swindled" one day while she was hanging around near home. She was often outside because her parents were away all day for work.

One day, the man living in the same building, a person she knew very well, told her that he had brought home a beautiful puppy and asked her to follow him so she could make friends with the puppy.

Mr. Rossi was really a good friend to her and she was glad when he paid her attention. The attention that was lacking in her family.

Cl. ...*I was very happy, I always wished to have a doggy,*

but my parents always said no, because it would have been a problem when they were away. Mr Rossi was always kind and friendly to me. He would often stop and joke with me. We went up to his flat… and there he took advantage of me…

June said the molestation went on for some time. *"When I used to see him I remember I would get frozen and paralyzed and just follow him".*

Now Jane "is reiterating" her abuser's pattern. In therapy with violent clients, I noticed "what triggers" this specific pattern is the ancient cry to the caregiver: "NO! I WON'T give up", **I cannot accept being defeated, because I am innocent and deserve what I need.**

Here she is not a victim… but a sort of "abuser"… this is a safe (destructive) way to avoid pain, terror and loss and the "stubborn/revenging" feeling of being innocent. When these feelings and emotions are **removed/denied** from the conscious world, the victim is destined to repeat the abuser's behaviour.

Short circuit

Let us now go back again to the statement made at the beginning:

The child's experience is paralyzing on two levels… one concerns the distortion of the "inner" being–in-the-world (*the expectation*)… the other has to do with the experience of abuse/trauma in itself. (*What really happened*).

So this means that experiences of sexual abuse, besides causing a trauma for the event, also contain the **expectation of satisfying certain needs.** (Bosio)

But need is UNSATISFIED and FROZEN by the abuse.

The unsatisfied need is *an experiential void* and *uncompleted act* that keeps on claiming its fulfilment, and causes:

* A "compulsive reiteration", as Freud would say.

* A "drive" as Maslow would say.

* An "uncompleted existential act", existential philosophy would say

* An "interruption in the actualizing tendency" as Rogers would say.

* An "energy at the mercy of a void", that strives to "grasp" something, says biology.

In fact, also in biology an open chain will search outside the chain, for other fragments to close the chain.

* A "black hole", says quantic theory. Two energies with different frequency.

* An area of the brain that triggers the symbolized process, says neuroscience

I've pointed out all this evidence to prove the validity of my statement that: it is the **incomplete existential act;** the un-finished that does not allow the closing of the circle. It is the I-Me. It is the "emotional world" that holds everything at stake.

The outcome is that besides the healing of the sexual wound, there is an unresolved "behavioural pattern" giving way to the "reiteration" of an abusive experience. This means that a complete healing of abuse needs to go back to a recovery in the child's life history. "Unfinished business" says George de Rita.

I shall try to explain the "trap" with fragments of a few therapeutic sessions.

Mandy: (mentioned above).
Mandy has found out that what triggers her

reiteration, or getting back into the loop of abuse is receiving "ATTENTION"… The need to **"belong"** to someone. Here we are in the realm of an ancient dream-need, back into her life history.

Her family had a very close friend, John, often invited for lunch on Sundays. He used to come along with presents for her and her brother and sometimes would play games with her.

"He paid special attention to me, used to keep me on his lap and play with me". (Says the client). *He was the only person giving me attention, the attention I was always looking for. One day he asked my mother if after lunch, he could take me to the movies to see Bugs Bunny: I was excited and very happy. I got into the car and was so happy… but he went to a near highway. Stopped the car and abused me…"*

Which were Mandy's expectations and feelings towards him? They were very different:

Oh! Beautiful! He is caring towards me. Taking me to the movies! He satisfies my need… a craving for ATTENTION and love…

Here are the child's expectation and the man's promise…

But, the promise, is betrayed - Mandy's existential act is not completed – her need/dream once more **overlooked,** but also **betrayed** – the existential act isn't "actualized". Moreover, burdened with a sexual experience. Theory says "An act has a beginning and an end". When it's realized/actualized, it makes a "circle" that is added to the "chain of life" that determines my story in the stream of life. In this case, the circle is broken and at one end, there is an uncompleted act/experience of "what was supposed to be", at the other end of the circle a "new" and unexpected traumatic experience.

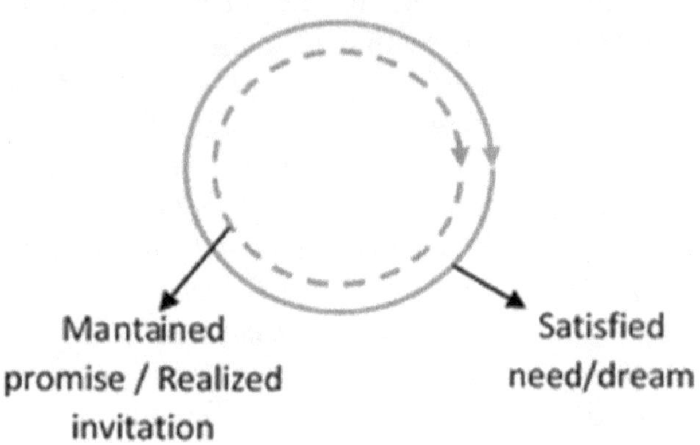

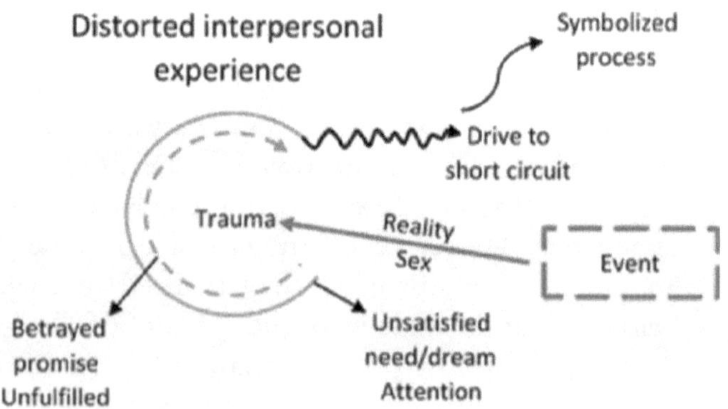

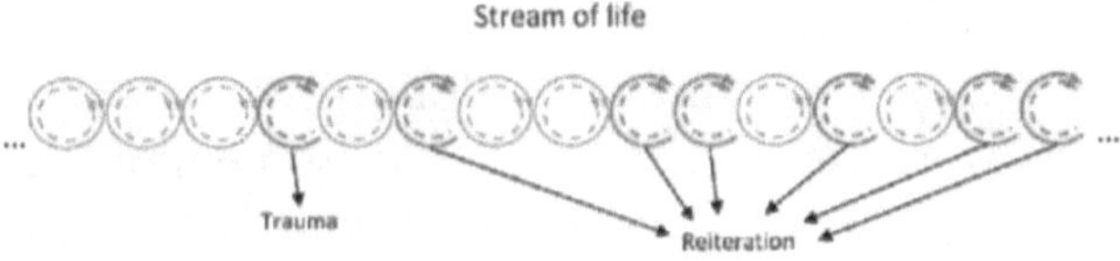

Adulthood

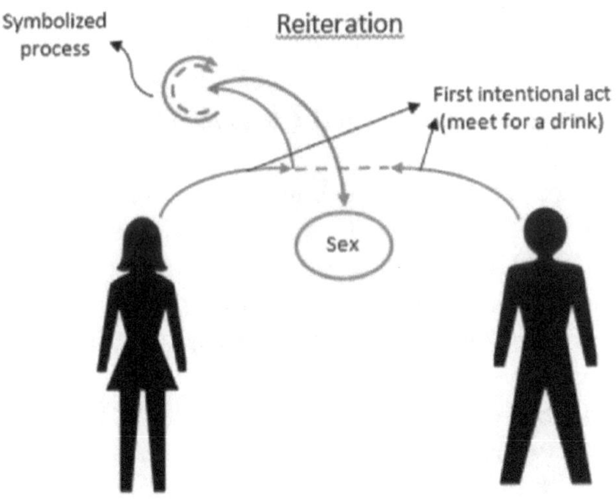

An area of the brain triggers the symbolized process

Given these explanations, let us go back to Mandy and to her process.

Mandy went through a long psychotherapy and has overcome her trauma but something else is "keeping" her in the trap; "*something is keeping me there*", she says.

After a few months from this session, she receives a phone call from her friend Tom (who shows up now and then)... and she gives up again... "*even though I had said to myself that I wouldn't yield to his sexual requests*" says Mandy. They met and "made love for hours"...

In the session, Mandy says:

Cl. *I never made love being so entirely myself...*

Th. *Seems that something changed...*

Cl. *He paid me so much loving attention, always telling me to feel at ease...to let go...*

Th. *He had never done that... or said so?...*

Cl. *No... no... never. I was different too... I wanted to do something for myself...* **I felt I was there...**

Two weeks later she comes to her session: she says that he called again. This is what she brings into the session. The following are fragments of the session:

Cl. *He calls me on the phone. We have a chat and he says, "Fix yourself up in such and such a way"* (she does not say what he wants her to do).

After the call, I say to myself... no... I'm not going to do that... no... not at all. What does he think?... no... go on...Ok I'll do it... no, no...and so on...

Th. *It seems he makes you do it?... and your feelings have ups and downs.*

Cl. *...I feel that he pays me such special attention.*

Th. *Attention!* (I exclaim. She looks up at me... eyes into eyes... silence...)

Th. *There you are... John...!* (Her childhood abuser)

Cl. *This time I felt like I was a prostitute... there you are!* (She is putting fragments together... I wait...)

Cl. *There you are... It's me who believes he pays me caring attention... I am only an instrument for him... playing sex... just like Andrew* (another abusive lover) *used to do...We used to play with our smartphones exchanging sexual performances and fantasies...That is what Tom asked me to do... He asks me "did you reach orgasm?"... I was shocked... I remembered Andrew...*

The day after Tom calls me: "send me some photos...what would you like to send me?... what would you like to do?..." I do not answer... I did not know what to say...

(I see her expression is changing, and I slip in, voicing a "felt meaning")

Th. *You are confused...*

Cl. *...He says to me "do something... How? What?" I answer: "I am confused"* (she is talking in the present tense, this means she is "in" the scene)*... I reply: "I do not know what to say...* (She is calling for help, like a child)*... "Say something", he answers me... "show me your clitoris..." I'll show you my clitoris...no, no... "what's happening?" he asks me... "What are you thinking? Let me see you having an orgasm". He goes on asking me... I put a hand on my pubes... suddenly I remember Andrew...*

The day after I send Tom a message and ask him: "What kind of interest do you have in me?... watch out how you answer, 'cause you could lose me". He didn't answer.

(I remain silent while she goes on talking but I keep close to what she is saying and feeling... I am letting her loose but she knows I am there with her)

"But the day after, he calls and says: I am near your home ... do this, this and that, and when you open the door show up with your eyes blindfolded... And it all ends up in bed..."

(Silence…) *I understand that I don't exist for him… only a fetish… fetish* (looks up into my eyes) *how will I be able to change?…*

Th. …*For now, it's important to notice that "attention, interest" no longer have the taste of tenderness, warmth, attention; of belonging to him, but as a prostitute. Just stay in the "here and now". That's how you are feeling… how you are* (I am showing here with my attitude and answer that I am in "that" reality… that's how things are… ok… let us stay there, don't worry… somewhere "we" shall go… I feel I'm soothing her troubled waters, accepting what is going on… I am here with you… by your side…)

Cl. *And I discovered that I reach orgasm if I **"think"** that my partner is paying **"attention"**… I, as regards myself, don't exist…my focus is only on the other…*

(Unfolding threads slowly embodied into a healing self…)

A LATER SESSION:

Cl. *I feel that I must "close" some wounds. I sent a message to Andrew. This is what I wrote, A long time ago you asked me if our story was going through the flu or if it was cancer… I didn't answer you. Now, I shall answer… cancer… Yes, it was a cancer…*

Then there is Tom… What keeps me tied to him? He has nothing… Nevertheless I am there… I keep thinking… and suddenly… I remembered a dream: I was with him making love. A very deep, whole, full feeling. It was totalizing… This was the dream I was recalling the morning after… and in a loud voice, I shouted "Mandy I love you"… and there came a click! With each hand, she makes a circle with her fingers and puts them together… (OO)

That is me and my love (O) and him with his… (O)

The day after our meeting I wrote to him and told him how happy I was feeling: "It was wonderful... making love... I would like to do it again... I wonder... maybe we could get into something deeper, something else... are you interested?"... The answer that came back was "There is this... and only this"... And **"in that moment",** *something closed down in me*

Th. ...***The interest...***

Cl. *Yes... I with* **my** *love and him, with* **his** *interest... and it is sex and nothing... Me on one side; something as a Whole. On the other, there is a different "piece"... a fragment... not mine... but it is there...*

In **my interest,** *there is a total acceptance: love and sex. On the other side, I have been a "fragment" for the other person... his interest is only sex.*

Th. *You wanted something more...*

Cl. *I would have liked to hear: "Mandy I love you".*

Th. *That's what you have been dreaming*

Cl. *Yes...* (Silence...) *with John...* **I was dreaming of the movies, that he could be lovingly and caring towards me...** (The dream-need)

Th. ***A movie that did not arrive...***

Cl. *Yes Lovingness that was not there... he robbed me of something... his interest was not mine...he stole my dream...*

Th. *The healthy fulfilment of a dream* (she is innocent)

Cl. ...(Cries...) *The love that he was not supposed to give me. A love that was supposed to come from my mother and my father only.*

Th. ***A love that nobody else can give you...*** (I made a shift into the pages of her story. Another piece of the puzzle she has been facing).

Cl. *Yes... because it is a special love... a "Perfect Circle"... in one direction... I trusted him and he annihilated me…* (she took my cue and compared the two realities: the child and the caregivers - the child and John, her childhood abuser)

Th. *It's **here where** your expectations and your desire are suspended, interrupted. A game that remained "open"* (I designed a circle, open at both ends)

Cl. *And that is what I keep on doing… keep on looking for. Makes me go on and on again… it is always **that** damn dream… And I get into trouble when I feel "left alone".*
The childhood fear of being forsaken.

THE FOLLOWING SESSION:
Cl. *…I feel I'm in a "state of change"…something has broken… I feel I am getting out from under the "cloud" …The cloud is the dream…I had figured it as a cloud "popping up above my head".* ("strawberry ice cream").

Previously I had made a design for the client: the dream, the expectation, the betrayal, the "open" cloud… I was sure she was able to "follow me" since she had experienced it and went into this experiencing many and many a time. I use this in the right place and right time. A "time" that comes up spontaneously "in empathy" with the client…

Cl. *The fragment that has always been with me… it is always there…another part of me… but not mine… it is his…* (It is the same attention, but two different tastes!)

Th. *The one that always triggered your dream…*

Cl. *Yes… **the interest/attention for me**…* (The child's "attention: lovingness". The offender's "attention": sex. This is what the fragment is made of)

Th. *The string that kept you linked with your dream…*

Cl. *But he had "another dream"… hidden in "his" kind of interest for me…*

Th. *Yes, but you couldn't see that because you always saw him with* **"eyes of innocence"**...

Cl. *...Now that interest is for myself... I am the one who must give it to me... feel it "incarnated"...*

It was amazing, for the therapist in me, experiencing the "gathering" of pieces of the puzzle, into a harmonic design. The pieces being given a name in order to find their place in the concept of the Self.

So I can firmly state and recognize this "paradox" of the **Client Centred approach: If you allow the client "to flow" along realms of history and day-by-day life, he will gradually reach the ocean of actualizing tendency.**

I remember that once, I explained this non-directive way of working to a client. "This is an algorithm", she said. On a map, we can reach point B starting from point A, in a totally random way, with the only constraint of not going along the same way more than once, with the only opportunity to turn back. This journey could take an indefinite time. It proves that soon or later we reach the destination!

The therapist is the warm and reflecting "ego" of the person (the client), who knows his story, but cannot see, and I the therapist who doesn't know the story but can see... I help regain sight, thus facilitating self-regulation.

There is one thing I should like to find out and ask neuroscientists: **Where is the "craving dream" in the brain?...**

A few weeks later in another session, Mandy says:

The other day I was thinking about my experience. I clearly felt that Tom has no interest in me: he only wants to use me. This is what everybody has always done to me… I said to myself, How about calling Tom?… I could call… just to see what would happen… but there was no "click"… there was no click. Then I remembered Andrew, but also there, no click.

Nobody is waiting for me. I understand that I must go ahead on my own and **take care of myself***…*

As regards this aspect, I argued with my husband .We were talking about spaces to use at home. I needed a space for my job, in a certain room. It was the only thing I needed, but he wanted to use it for other things that didn't fit in with mine. For the first time, I started arguing. He said, "Well, that's it! Just manage to get it like this!" At this point a storm came rolling up in my body and I emptied myself of all I had been accepting and keeping inside during these three years with him… (She is taking hold of her "personal power"!)

Mandy went on explaining what happened. Eventually it turned out that he understood what she had been accepting and things started changing.

The session goes on and she says:

Cl. *And that thing hanging above* (she shapes with her fingers an open circle)

Th. (I smile)… *Yes the expectation…*

Cl. *It's no longer there! With my colleagues, too, I am no longer willing to accept to the decisions they take for me.*

A few months later in a session, she says:

Cl. …*the other day I was thinking about Tom and I looked him up on Facebook. He was with a friend I know. …and he was there…* **Yes he was "there", I was "here"***… I mean he was no longer "in the cloud"* (the dream)…was no longer there… I had sort of taken it in… not a cloud, but **reality**. **Now** he is nothing for me… I have never been anything for him…

This is another proof that the unfulfilled existential act is responsible for the reiteration of distorted patterns.

Later on Mandy gave me a card on which she had written:

The rescue or "safe nest" is a defence mechanism, just like when I am sad, I drink and sadness disappears. When I am afraid, I take refuge in a safe place in my mind. I go to a safe place and reality is "bypassed". It is a shelter from powerful feelings. A shield from fear or painful feelings, from threatening feelings, but reality is always there and soon or later, it will appear...

Mandy started walking on her own and called for a session when she needed to share an experience and put pieces in their right place in order to strengthen her personal power and be more assertive. In one of her last sessions, she reports another discussion with her husband and standing up for her ideas. She said to him *"I am no longer a Geisha... this upset him... but I held on to my power... He did not speak to me for the whole day. I felt the pain of being "shut out" from his world. Suddenly Tom turned up in my mind* (loneliness and "not belonging to" tracked her back...) *but I didn't feel anything of the kind "now I'll call Tom", because I saw him with my **"eyes of reality"**. I felt I was safe.*

This is proof of the validity of all this work.

Three months later Mandy calls for another session.

Cl. *...I argued with my husband... He did not want to listen to me and kept on saying it's impossible to talk, recently I* *can't say anything to you without quarrelling. Of course, I replied, I no longer accept your bossing me. I felt sick when I said this and my mind went to Tom... and Andrew... but they don't exist anymore.*

I noticed her pleasure and surprise.

Th. *Of course, the short circuit is closed! It doesn't work anymore.*

Mandy's wide eyes are surprised.

Cl. *How did it close?*

Th. *No longer craving attention. Your attention is focused on yourself, so when necessary, you react.*

Cl. *Yes! It works! Now I see there are holes where once there were these needs. I have to fill them up...*

Th. *Sure!*

Surprised eyes. Waiting for an answer...

Th. *There is the little girl with her Actualizing Tendency waiting for you.*

Cl. *Yes. Where John molested me. That was not me. I was there waiting for something else.*

Th. *Craving for lovingness and safe attention...* **there where the Dream of life began.**

As we can notice in this brief fragment of the session, the interaction between therapist and client has changed. The dialogue changes. The energy levels are becoming similar.

Another Example: Always in the same trap. A pattern to change.

Anita, a very skilful medical doctor... The following is what she brings to a session.

Cl. *This morning my head physician came to the ward, where I was visiting the patients and told me that he had spoken to some of his colleagues in different wards and found another position for me in the social work department... you could move there, he said, so you won't have any more problems with your colleagues.*

Th. *Aren't you preparing papers and documents for a promotion to head physician?*

Cl *Yes...*

Entangled in her trap!... No reaction coming from her side...

In an instant, my inner world turned upside down! Pictures of Anita's story came rolling through my mind:

Some years ago, she was working in a ward for anorexic adolescents in another hospital, working on a project she herself had set up. Once she succeeded in bringing these girls to a restaurant for a pizza! The head physician was astonished... he called her interested in how she had been so successful with these girls... The obedient "little girl" explained everything. She didn't care about being clever, she was only *"craving" to be accepted,* not neglected... A few weeks later he moved her to the paediatric ward in a different hospital where she is now working. Her project went ahead with the doctors of his team...

All this came up at once and I could not help uttering a cry. Of the type fear -attack!

Th. *He is a wolf... he is cheating you!*

I was reading and reflecting in a bath of emotions and crude reality; I just dived, holding her, into reality...

Th. *He does not want you to go for the promotion...*

She froze... **cuddled up like a child** and with a humble smile, her shoulders in the posture of wanting to hide... She said, in a whisper...

Cl. *He is like my brother..."* (her childhood abuser)

Tears welled up in my eyes...

Cl. (Tears roll down her cheeks…) *I always believe in their protecting me… I hang onto them. Like onto my doggy's neck. I walk along trusting him… them… and they lead me into their den…*

Th. *It's* **your craving** *for love and protection…*

Cl. *I give everything… and they cheat me…*

Th. *You do not see the wolf… your eyes look with* **"eyes of innocence"***…*

I then explained what she had been experiencing, by describing the "loop", so she could easily track with me **her way of being,** since she had experienced it.

(She has been in therapy for a few years). I explained and designed the **"uncompleted existential act"** and **"the abuse"** that gives way to the **"short-circuit".**

Th. *You have been looking with your eyes of innocence.*

Cl. *Oh yes!…* (She touches her eyes and says)… *Yes. Yes now I see "After"…*

Yes… this "after" means: the "behind" has come to end… it is behind… now I am in "the now"… (I was astonished and amazed).

During these years of psychotherapy, Anita had mentioned an abuse suffered by her brother, but never went into details. I always respected this closure.

This session became the outpouring of what her "Newfoundland" big doggy- brother did to her…a little child at the mercy of herself dealing with a brother who was her "protector"… since she was rejected by her caregivers, but also her abuser.

When a child, she was "too clever"… this overshadowed her brother, mummy's pet, with all the consequences. Her father was depressed. *"When home from work, we had to be quiet otherwise he would go crazy at us".* Anita was disregarded by both parents. *"My brother had to take care of me. Mum used to say that he had to protect me. I could not go out without him".*

She was eight years old when he started abusing her (he was 12) up to when he began dating girls.

Th. He was like a big doggy… a Newfoundland…and you the little sister hanging on to his neck totally relying upon him…

These sessions are the evidence that differently abused "wounds" are healed, ***getting through the emotional world***

As regards body feelings and postures, both Mandy and Anita made a change.

Mandy:

Mandy felt a "sort of skin" slightly covering her, a feeling of "warm protection". Her relation to the outside world: *"I feel more focused within myself…and there is a new sort of a distance between me and others…a space between us"* (her **living-space** recovered). Her eyes are no longer those of a "paralyzed frightened animal".

The following is an incredible coincidence!

I said to her *"I see in your eyes a sea with waves calming down…before there were sort of "crispy waves"…* She looks at me in astonishment…

Cl. That takes me back to long ago… At the specialization school of sex therapy, you were my teacher at clinical classes. We performed a role-play. I do not remember if I was the client or therapist… At the end of the role-play, you asked for feedback on the experience. We worked it out. Then you asked me how I was feeling. I answered. You came near me, put a light hand on my shoulder and said: "there is the *calm before the storm"… and the storm did come!… and that's why I chose you as my therapist some years later…And now you are saying to me: **"the Calm after a Storm"**…*

Anita:
Anita changed her voice, the rhythm of her speaking…no longer the cry of a mourning baby. She walks shoulders back. No longer like a little girl walking shoulders bent. She no longer has a shy face and now looks into one's eyes…

Their emotional world is sending new signals, different feelings, different **"Ways of Being"**… So… The way "Out" is: "Through". In neurosciences it is a "cooling down".

With the aid of existential philosophy, I notice a difference between human behaviour and animal behaviour. The only way to help an animal with "emotional" or behavioural problems is with "conditioning" exercises.

The way out with humans, can be through exercises for a certain kind of uneasiness, but a "total" resilience goes ***through consciousness and feelings*** and ***"distorted" expectations***, voicing **hidden pieces** of one's experience, "unfinished business" that creeps into many of our daily behaviours. All is traced back to the Person's personal and "subjective" world; using the Person's "Frame of Reference". (Rogers)

Angie
Angie came to me because she wanted to know why she always fails with the men with whom she sets up a relationship.

"It is the fourth time I've made plans to set up a family, but suddenly I feel I "have nothing to do" with that person…"

A beautiful woman gifted with both aspects of strength and delicacy - straightforward and romantic - intellectual and sensitive. A nice image of "yin and yang". After a while, she talks about abuse. Incest started when she was a child and went on up to adolescence.

Working on her interacting with men, it turns out that she often has an attitude of the kind: "I am a little girl... take me with you... please take me in your arms". Her voice also changes into a "twittering child". A dear friend of hers told her that when they are in a group with friends, she notices that sometimes Angie switches over into a "chirping attractive little girl".

She also realizes that when she relates to men with a certain look: strong, attractive, caring, she automatically changes her gaze. It turns into a deep, penetrating, seductive look. (All this came out by "focusing" (Gendlin) on the contents she brought to therapy).

"There is something that attracts me..." We move and go deeper into this experiencing in order to bring feelings, emotions, memories to the surface and it turns out that **"her heart sinks into the eyes of the lonely loser and lets herself be taken"**. *"There is a part of me that says to myself: "where are you going? Do you really want to stay with this person? Do you want to quit? But nevertheless I stay there... like in trance... Later on I realize I have nothing to do with my partner and it takes me a long time to split up"*

Little by little, (that is, after other sessions) she realizes that these glances occur occasionally in her daily life: with the butcher, with the waiter in the coffee shop near home, but she "quickly" leaves the place. She is becoming more aware of her way of being. Now, she understands the "distance" she keeps between herself and others. *"Now I realize how icy I am and I don't like this"*. I gave her a warm return explaining that, "it was the only way she had found to protect herself". Her "icy way" needed respect and before changing that attitude, there were wounds to heal. (This is "staying with the client's frame of reference" in that precise moment, and respecting her "way of being"; for the moment she can only behave in such a way, and it is ok.

In her sexual life, she behaves like a little child: *"I speak with a childish voice and cuddle up and let things happen. There is only this part... no orgasm... I am somewhere else"*.

Recently she happens to meet her ex - partner and a deep feeling of hatred springs up at once. She feels guilty because *"he wasn't his fault if we split up... I do not understand what his presence stirs up in me"*.

I invite her to go into the topic: "shall we try to see what this hatred is about?" After a while, she says, *"I hate his pain. I hate the sadness in his eyes. I hate the emptiness of his life... I cannot bear his look. I struggle to avoid those eyes"*. I add. "a desert of silence and solitude"... (That was what her eyes were reflecting in that moment). Silence... I immediately went on. "Where does your desert of loneliness, of solitude, of eternal silence come from?"... She answers: "It belongs to my mother". I reply. "Yes, it could be... a child can feel the depression and loneliness of a caregiver, when the other caregiver is of no help". I could say this because I knew her story, so I used it as a prompt. She goes: *"They were and still are, two people living on their own under the same roof. My father reacts with his aggressive words, but I see his isolation, his inability to socialize. My mother always at home… never had friends… goes out only to buy food… she keeps on cooking… nobody speaks".* I have also a sister.

I just reflect a felt meaning: "A world of distance, of silence and solitude". Tears well up in her eyes… *"Yes …and when I meet men with something like this in their eyes I feel sick…".* This is new because so far she has been using the defense mechanism or **"acting out"** the "attractive woman". Her true inner world is connecting with her!… *The feeling I had and still have towards my father… Why?*

Now I try to go deeper; she is in touch with her authentic reality, in touch with her **inner child,** the parts of the Self she has been hiding under her acting out. I say "The desert and solitude of those eyes might also belong to you… somewhere inside…" She is there with me… *"how can I find out?"* I answer "Let's see…What happens inside you just before you get into that hypnotic/seductive state of being?...when you surrender to the other person"?... Her reply: *"I see the desert of solitude; of being left alone…it kills me".* I go on. I go deeper… "This feeling comes from far away… it's your little girl…" She makes a link: *"This is when I get into Stephen's arms (her new partner) and start speaking like a child… and he is the one who looks more than anyone else like my father…"*

Angie always said, she was not able to hate her father and was ashamed of this… after all he had done to her… I never gave any answer, since I had no answers. Her father would take her, hand in hand, and go down stairs to the cellar to get bottles of wine and oil and once there he would molest her. In that session I said: " that little girl so lonely and sad met the little boy (her father's inner child) with those eyes that were eyes looking into a lonely desert, just like your eyes at the moment… **your heart longing for warmth met the lonely boy in your father's eyes"**. Tears went silently rolling down her face.

After this session she decided to go back home because she wanted to embrace her father after 20 years. She did it and felt that some pieces of the puzzle joined. When she hugged him, she allowed silent tears wet her face. Her father did not move but was touched by what was going on.

During her stay, they went down to the cellar again to get the oil. Her mother was present and immediately asked Angie anxiously: "shall I come with you?" When she came back, maybe she was deep into her feelings and her mother suddenly asked her in anxiety "what happened?"… "Nothing!" replied Angie. "Are you ok?" asked mother. "Yes!" Angie replied and in that moment she understood that the doubt she had been holding all those years, came true… mother always knew… Another piece had found its place in her inner world.

Angie spent three years of hard work on herself before reaching the depths of her childhood experiences. She is still working in order to give dignity and recognition to all her painful experiences. So far we haven't discovered *the uncompleted existential act that triggers the short-circuit.*

Some weeks later:
The session begins with Angie complaining because she keeps on thinking about her feelings of hatred when she met Marc recently.

Cl. *When he comes to my mind, I keep on getting angry.*

Th. I reply. *I remember you said your sadness meets his… how come?*

Cl. *I don't know… now I also hate thinking about sex with him, it is disgusting…*

Th. *When you met him this did not happen… something held you there…*

Cl. *Yes…*

I asked myself what triggered her …what "kept/trapped" her there? I tried to summarize some pieces of the puzzle:

Th. "You ran away from the butcher-you ran away from the waiter of the coffee shop- you ran away from the yoga teacher… with whom you had **sexualized attitudes… whereas with Marc something keeps you there…**

Where is the short circuit? …Let me see. Now I am going to think "aloud", so you can follow me". I began thinking and speaking. I was keeping her in an empathic touch with me, following my "thinking": "Well… You say you have a sexualized attitude… Sometimes you run away to avoid this… Children who are abused, sometimes, since they cannot or are afraid to speak, their body talks to the world for them: they lift up their dresses; pull down their knickers or **perform sexual behaviours**… It is the so called "acting-out"… natural consequences in abused children…

Cl. *That's what I did!* (She shouts out).

I did not say anything and went on "thinking" but "that" was another and a new, important piece of the puzzle…

Th. *Oh, you used to have sexualized attitudes, is that what you mean?*

Cl. *Yes*

Th. *Got it!... your sexualized behaviour is now, your sexualized look... But how come with your father?... You* **use***d this* **behaviour only** *in the world... trying to explain your uneasiness.* (It is an acting out) *Now your* **eyes** *are* **sexualized** *"after" meeting a man's sad eyes...*

Cl. *Yes...*

Th. *You once told me that your eyes send a message that is: "I'm a little girl... take me in your arms..."*

Cl. *This is what I am doing now with Stephen and he does it...*

Th. *Like what your father did...*

Cl. *Yes...*

Th. *Where is the short circuit? ...What brought you towards him "before" all this?* **His solitude***... you say ...the "solitude" you met in his eyes... The "solitude" that yesterday led you towards the colleague at the course.* (She attended a course for her business)

Cl. *Yes ...I couldn't bear to see her all alone in a city that she didn't know and had to wait till late before leaving on a bus and travel all night.*

Th. *Seems you felt a sort of solitude in her, she was alone, in a city she didn't know.* Cl. *Yes ...I felt the need to help her.*

Th. *You could not bear to see your father alone, not considered. You wanted to take care of him, so* **you kindly paid him attention ...but he betrayed you...**

Her body turned stiff while tears welled up into her sad and terrified eyes. I wanted to make her understand that these things "can" happen... Thus, I told her the "story" of another little girl. (This is "sharing or confrontation" used in encounter groups).

Th. "I remember a client who told me that when she was little, her dad would come home very late. He had an important business to manage. Her mother, a highly depressed and angry woman, would ignore him. Hence, the daughter would go and fetch his slippers and sit at the table while he was having dinner. *"I felt he was so lonely and I was glad to stay with him"* the client said" ...Angie was staring at me with her wide beautiful eyes. **Eyes of a child hounded in a desert of solitude and pain... I asked her:**

Th. *Does this say something to you?*

Cl. *...Pieces of the stories of other children who did the same things...*

I understand her answer because in the work with abused women I often noticed that when they understand that they did nothing to cause the abuse, that it is not their fault, also Angie felt that she was not , or no longer "the only one", because many children become "the adult", in troubled families...

In this case, Angie, like the other little girl, projected on her father **"her feeling of loneliness, her feeling of being left alone, her feeling of being at the mercy of a wild world".**

Angie gave him what "She" was in need of... BUT... he betrayed her.

The session shifted toward her feelings of uneasiness in the family, her pain for the atmosphere of a world of *"stillness":* nobody spoke for hours. A world where lovingness was a *"cold desert".* Where a father would shout and grumble, when things went wrong. A mother that would answer only with her passive, silent, aggressive attitude. She was harsh and cold, never answered, stubborn in her *"motionless world".*

Th. *The lovingness and warmth you were craving for, you gave it to your father...*

Cl. *I always felt a tenderness towards my father, something... a common feeling...*

Th. *The hunger for love… desolation and solitude. Your inner child knew what she needed and is still in need and looking for that lovingness…*

Cl. *How can I get rid of her? I don't want her anymore…*

Th. *You cannot get rid of her. She is the one who carries her innocence, her creativity, her staying in the "here and now of life". She will always be looking for lovingness. You cannot rip this away from her. She has a magic thought. You adult are the one who knows reality, has a critical sense of reality. You know perfectly well, now, that your parents will never change. You have to "give up asking". It is the funeral of your "strawberry ice-cream".*

I saw her holding her breath. I quickly continue: **"It is from the ashes of this funeral that you shall be re-born…"**

She ended the session saying: **"I feel destroyed. But I know what you mean".**

From a scientific point of view, what happened? Let us see:

Angie comes complaining again about her hatred toward Marc, but something else is working "underwater"…

My hypothesis might be the following.

- The day before this session, she met the colleague who was alone at the workshop and this stirred up her "caregiver" attitude: *"I saw her alone. She didn't know anybody around her. She had to wait all alone for the coach for a long time and travel all night…* **So:**

- *The lady's* **sad eyes** went down to Angie's inner child's wounds and during the session they surfaced to consciousness (the desert around her, the hours of silence, the loneliness in making decisions).

- Her "sad eyes" taking care of the colleague **(Angie's inner child)** and later "Angie's sad eyes" meeting Marc **(the adult short-circuit).**

These "confrontations" enabled her to put important pieces of the puzzle together. My comment surely needs further evidence. Nevertheless, we must start from somewhere… So far, it works…

Some details which can shape client-centred therapy

COSMIC VIEW:

Cosmic view is not religion. These are "universal values" that can be found in nature, existentialism, physics, such as Respect, Loose ends, Matching ends, Limits, Opposites and so on.

DOUBT:

The greatest certainty in existential philosophy is "doubt": One must accept life with an attitude that includes doubt. That is how I deal with clients in the therapeutic process: "…where can I go now…" asks the client. "I do not know", is my answer. "We can just go ahead or stay (in the client's present reality)". These are the only two certain things we have: "where we are now… and making a choice with the concept of *doubt*". When I say this, conveying *"let it be, the present is the "step" that will lead us somewhere"*, the client utters a sigh of relief. They understand that there is no need to move, so they turn their "focus" back to the "here and now".

A successful therapy puts and end to the questioning of the meaning of existence. Once we have accepted the "limits of being," live in the stream of life and have come to terms with the philosophical meaning of "nothing", we shall stop looking forward. Everything is relative – precarious – impermanent – limited, so: there is nothing to lose and we live in the "here and now".

"Freedom is just another word for nothing else to lose"
Janis Joplin

UNCONDITIONAL POSITIVE REGARD:

It is "withholding judgement". It is possible because the therapist **is in** the client's "frame of reference". It is "empathizing and staying with the client's congruency". Thus, the therapist's congruency falls apart as regards inner values.

This means relating with the client as a PERSON and being in touch with the "universal ethical value of RESPECT" which says I respect you as a human being. This means respect for the person in spite of all the "empirical evidence" (unworthiness), through contact with an "essential self" worthy of respect.

Respect is a universal value that leaves the person with "dignity"

<u>FRAME OF REFERENCE</u>

It is the subjective perception of a person's inner and outside world. Rogerian therapy moves along this pathway, in a non-directive manner. Sometimes the therapist might use other "tools" such as confrontation, interpretation when required in specific situations.

I want to conclude this work by showing how valuable it is to stay "with the client's "Frame of

Reference".

Joseph.

A client who has been in therapy for 5 years.

A few months earlier, he split up with his girl-friend in whom he had invested all his love and life.

Pieces from a session

Cl. *I am in terrible pain… and fear. There is a black place before me. I don't want to go there. I am scared* (crying) *I can't stay there …I'll go crazy…*

Th. *Looking ahead is frightening… you are scared to move on… try to stay there where you are now, with the pain… it's your reality. The pain that you are now feeling is real. You have lost Giulia and this is painful.*

Cl. *It takes me back to my dad, to when he would belt me and reduce me to a pin, nothing but a pin… All around me was dark, just like now. I was scared… I could go crazy… I was nothing. Reduced to a cell… Can you understand? Now this can lead me to a breakdown…* <u>(This is his frame of reference. Here I start a focusing on this point)</u>.

Th. <u>*That single cell saved you and is now saving you. It's pure energy/light and it will not die out. Stay with that pin or cell. This is your reality: a cell, a pin.*</u> *Stay with your pin.* **It will** *take you hand in hand and, step by step when you are ready to move, will lead you out toward the light.*

That evening he sent a message in English: "I am doing it. My little sun goes shining. Thanks for existing by my side".

This statement reminds me of a poem:

The Search –
My love… tell me what you need
Oh yes! the sweet voice tenderly says:
My love… love tell me what you want
Love tell me what I can do for you

I am here… I am listening to you
I am here… I care for you
Oh yes my love… I'm waiting for you
A dream vanished through time but,
I meet it again in this moment.
Now… to myself
From: A psychotherapy? No a Lifetime

TRACING THE CLIENT'S PATHWAY:

That is "keeping in touch". Empathy works when the therapist connects with client's frame of reference. It consists of "tracing" his/her pathway avoiding interpretations which shift attention from feelings to intellectualization. Interpretation is "staying outside" the client's world. You can also tell someone to "forget", but words and mind do not solve the problem (Gestalt). To leave past and pains "behind" but they will come "in front of you". One can experience "grieving" (psychodrama) but atonement does not solve the problem.

The most remarkable grieving is the "Void" caused by the "not given" and that one keeps on searching. The Void works hopelessly in *short-circuits* and in *working on dreams* (strawberry ice cream). (Bosio)

ACTUALIZING TENDENCY:

The organismic tendency to develop all the potentialities to build patterns and behaviours necessary for the developing organism to move towards autonomy and away from heteronomy or control by outside powers. Hindering it, it causes destructive reactions for the organism.

SELFCONSCIOUSNESS:

Is an authentic dwelling with the "essence" of Self.

An "inner" instrument firmly anchored to daily life. The opposite of conformism. It "works" linked to the organismic self, in collaboration with one's actualizing tendency that deals in congruency with the inner world that "seeks" to be in congruency with the outside world.

Chapter 4 - From the dark depths of being to the skies of freedom

Fragments validating the process.

Validation can only come from the clients' experiencing.

Wendy.

This is a text message Wendy sent me. Her therapy is almost coming to the end.

I received the photos of the day I discussed my thesis. When I saw the photo of the hug the director of the course gave me at the proclamation, I cried. My father's embraces always turn into a joke rejecting me. It is such an ancient deep pain that maybe I've been able to get in touch with it now. I should like to be loved, well treated, not rejected. This comes even before my concern at being searched by filthy hands.

I answered:

Attention is the dream built upon the experience of the **"not given"**. **"Being rejected"** is the **wound**.

After some days she wrote for a session and added:

I often bear within me the words of your last message.

I answered:

Yes, my dear it is a wound that goes down into the deepest parts of your roots. Hold that embrace dear.

The Dark:

Mandy is now in touch with the depths where lies the "Being" of the child: "little Mandy". The little girl, who is hurt, wounded, not considered, rejected. The sorrow for the "not given". The ancient pain for the wounds she suffered. She is **lonely**, in the dark among her wounds. The dreaded feeling of a lonely child. A child cannot but feel alone having no caregiver to contain her feelings and having no tools to be self-sufficient... "to fly". Now Mandy has found her. At present, this is what Mandy is feeling.

The Light:

Now I shall swap over to fragments of another client who is dealing exactly with those "pieces in loneliness".

Jim.

A childhood of physical abuse by his father and an absent mother: "impalpable", he says.

J: *...I am trying to stay ...I am staying with my pain...* (He usually "stops/blocks" the feeling because he gets scared; an emotion that turns into a feeling of violence).

Th: ... ... silence

J: *How can I get rid of my pain?...*

Th: silence... (I am just staying with him. I don't want to break his feelings)

J: *It will be always there. I must accept it.*

Th: you must accept its Reality... your pain is the **"not given"**... the being **"unfairly punished"**...

J: ... ... crying.

He is here with me in his loneliness, in his "here and now"... I must be careful not to become the substitute for his parents, even though I feel like hugging him. But, especially for a destructive person, it would be worse. It is dangerous: lovingness goes straight down to his wounds, deep to his hurting wounds. It deepens the pain that can turn into violence (*Love is my enemy* by Mario Isotti). He has often said to me "I don't want to look into your eyes... they... go down to my wounds... and can turn into violence".

Th: There is a lot of loneliness with you... but a child, your little boy cannot be otherwise... has no tools to be on his own. You had no tools to take care of yourself... only bird can fly on their own.

This metaphor came up to me, feeling his havoc. He was/we were surfacing from the depths of the "dark part" so I felt I could give him a motherly holding. Staying in empathy with him, it came up by association of ideas. For me, the therapist, it is possible since I am in the situation of: "As If" so I am just where he Is: his being in the here and now, but also "out of his frame of reference".

J: ...Yes, **I have lost the game**. The VERY FIRST time he has admitted this! (After a good number of years in therapy. His being innocent would not allow him to say "I lost the game").

Th: Yes my dear... (In a sad but soothing voice).

J: I can't expect Silvia (the girl he is dating) to give me those things. They would never be the taste of my parents' ...it would be a bottomless pit...

Overwhelmed he stands up and walks out of the room... Comes back.

Th: Yes my dear, it is true. But it will be beautiful

flapping your wings on your own, **UP INTO THE SKY**.

A beautiful smile crosses his face and eyes.

On the doorstep, he hugged me… stayed there for a while and said: "I feel I can hug you for a little while".

Conclusion

I feel I must end my work with this philosophical and psychological concept:

"Giving up needs and frustration leads to "compassion" and there is neither good nor evil but only Cosmic Love".

"It is in the ***"finitude"*** of the Being that the human sacrifice is accomplished and individuals regain that ***"spiritual"*** feeling that sets them free from the **"chains"** of Being…"

Cosmic love is a universal value. It has to do with "sharing", with respect toward oneself and others. In physics, a "black hole" has "respect" for a star moving toward it and produces/creates a "lifesaver" around itself. Losing energy; it reduces its destructive power, so that the star will not be devoured by the hole. Hence, they both streak across the universe in harmony and respect for each other saving the **beauty** of their being. Humanity also is equipped with a "safety distance": a space between us, and the world. A distance that should never be violated, not even by a caregiver, in the name of universal values. But often the landmark is trespassed on by abusers causing a disruption in the victims "existing".

Gregory Bateson:
The infinitely high
The depths of waters
The extreme and challenging complexity
of the multicellular
The apparent simplicity toward the unicellular
are all extreme elements of a unique equilibrium.

The following letter intended to be evidence that working with "empathy" and "frame of reference", leads to an actualizing tendency and hope towards an unknown future: existential philosophy.

****Dear Maddalena,*

I am writing this letter because I know, in spite of the long relationship we have had, I would not be able to say these things face to face.

I want to thank you, and for me, thanking is always a difficult thing, because I experience it with ambivalence. In your case, I am happy and I really want to tell you that, had it not been for you, I do not know what would have become of me and of my life.

In some moments, terrible for me, you were there. In other happy ones, too. You have always used ways that put me at ease, that made me feel accepted, not judged, or in some circumstances also spurred me on in a strong but never violent manner. I believe that behind the professional capacity there is also the humanity of a clever and positive person.

I feel embarrassed writing things that may be obvious, but for me they are very important: you helped me to look at things happening around me with different eyes. To believe in the strength and in reality according to my point of view, (I am still practicing on this) you helped me to find an equilibrium, necessary in order to not be afraid to change my life. The equilibrium necessary to face change and not stopping in the "known". You sustained me when I was really about to break down and in the worst of moments; in the days of darkness I was comforted by the thought that I could have called you (as sometimes happened): this feeling, in many occasions really kept me alive.

I do not know how to thank you for your support, your words, silences that helped me to grow up. Owing to you, I am now able to understand which people I wish being surrounded by, if I can make the choice, and sort out the limits that I must necessarily set up between me and the world outside in order not to be entrenched.

I am aware there would be much more work to do. Sometimes a little bit of fear takes me when I think that I cannot be near you during the next few years, but I also have a lot more trust in myself, because I really feel I have changed since the first time I entered your study.

You helped me to paint a nice piece of the "wall of my life" (a metaphor I use to explain the therapeutic process) and now I am on the verge of making one of my dreams come true. I'm leaving my homeland for my first job. For a while, I shall try to fly on my own.

There would be much more to tell you, but at this moment, emotion is too, too strong.

I promise I shall keep you informed as regards my work and about me personally in the foreign land. I do hope indeed to go toward a better place, more suited to me and that might give me hospitality forever. Otherwise to attain all the means needed to come back home.

Beyond whatever might be, (only life shall tell me) you shall always be in my mind and I shall always think about what you taught and conveyed to me with love.

The "drama"

We are always "strangers" in the world of others… but we want to enter… How?… with a strategy that will satisfy our ancient unsatisfied needs: to belong to - be adopted-submit-in symbiosis-in a fusion… and so on… Strategies that will always fail…

The "Power" of unfulfilled desires/needs is the "Root" of all man's slavery.

P. Levine

The "therapy"

Therapy is a string that we, clients, take in our hands in the therapist's study and carry everywhere… always… The string "works" also during the night, in our dreams.

In order to yield something, we must take it and interweave it with existence…

(Client)

The "journey"

"It's gonna be a long walk home"…

(Bruce Springsteen)…

"Spiritual Way of Being"

No frontiers of religion, my friends how desperately do we need to be loved and love. When Christ said that *"Man does not live by bread alone"* he spoke of "hunger". This hunger was not the hunger of the body. It was not the hunger for bread. He spoke of a hunger that begins deep down in the very depths of our being. He spoke of a need as vital as breath. He spoke of our hunger for love.

Love is something you and I must have. We must have it because our spirit feeds upon it. We must have it because without it we become weak and faint. Without love, our self-esteem weakens. Without love, our courage fails. Without love, we can no longer look out confidently at the world. We turn inward and begin to feed on our own personalities, and little by little, we destroy ourselves.

With it, we are creative. With it, we march tirelessly. With it and with it alone, we are able to sacrifice for others.

Chief Dan George
Native American

John Brown
Ma don't you remember when I went off to war.
I thought when I was there
God! What am I doing here?
I'm tryin' to kill somebody or die tryin'
But the thing that scared me most
Was when my enemy came close
And I saw that his face was just like mine
Oh God just like mine!

Bob Dylan

Love is a one-way road
Love, just like respect
is not taken, it is donated.

The author

Born in Australia. Graduated in Psychology at University of Padova – Italy. Four years at the Facilitator Development Institute in Rome where I specialized in Rogerian Therapy.

My teachers and tutors were Carl Rogers, Chuck Devonshire, George De Rita, Nat Ruskin, John Wood.

During the four years in Rome, my tutor was Chuck Devonshire to whom I owe a great deal for his sensitivity and great capacity to convey the "non-directive" approach and the fundamental concepts of Person-Centred Therapy. These professors come from the Centre for The Study of The Person University at La Jolla in San Diego, California.

For four more years, I attended a supervision group conducted by Chuck Devonshire, treasuring a great deal of experience firstly with him and later with George De Rita. In my profession I was able to get hold of those "threads" that lay deep within the person's history and that "desperately" surface from the depths and become protagonists of our way of being ("the distorted actualizing tendency"). From this experience comes my book of poems: "A psychotherapy?...No... A lifetime...". It is a collection of poems written by a client and is the witness that there is a pathway in the therapeutic process. How long and painful is the road to travel.

For many years, I have been professor for Clinical Sexology at the Centro Italiano di Sessuologia in collaboration with the Clinical Sexology Service at the department of Psychology University of Bologna.

For ten years, I taught sex education in secondary schools and later wrote a book: "The voyage of our sexual growth".

I have written works on sexual topics for scientific reviews.

With this book on psychotherapy, I am here with all the limits that I realize may emerge, but with the hope that someone will take them and use them in order to move forward with a scientific "hand" in the phenomenal "Being in the World".

The last chapter is an attempt to give some theoretical evidence as regards child abuse. For this piece of work my thanks goes to Mariagnese Cheli, responsible for the "Centre against child abuse" of the Azienda Sanitaria of Bologna.

Read *A Psychotherapy? No... A Lifetime...*

Sometimes the therapeutic journey brings up a strong need to "fix" its most significant stages. So it happens that the person discovers a poetic vein in speaking and narrating. It's owing to this, that a client was able to track a pathway, to write a story of sorrow and of memories, nice and unpleasant; that the protagonist of the therapeutic process caught in her memory, slowly, slowly. And equally slowly, slowly she shaped the emerging figures in the fog with the aid of her psychotherapist. This piece of work shall lead the reader into the secrets of a therapy that turns out to be the research of the "true" story of the childhood of everyone of us. Each poem testifies how difficult it is to recall the past, to rebuild it through the renewal of emotions, anguish, experienced and concealed, until you find their sense by means of a crude, maybe cruel rereading of reality. It's as if we have many pieces of a puzzle of which we have lost the picture.

Read *You shall thank your enemies and love your story*

The book explains and describes the pathways leading to neurotic behaviours, beginning from early years of life, when we set up behavioural patterns that turn out to be fallatious, as regard our needs as well as our interactions with others. There are dreams which are defensive constructions in the name of unsatisfied needs of our childhood; against realities and family dynamics too different and dangerous to cope with, in a developmental stage when a child has no instruments to face or deal with such "troubled waters". Certain fears in adulthood, overwhelming though irrational to intellect, are the outcome of those moments, when a child was unable to face reality, being at the mercy of oneself, impotent, thus in danger and without a protecting caregiver. In this healing process, shared with a psychotherapist, in a long and painful revisitation of what occured, the unveiling of an emotional world silenced long ago, we dismantle paths built with so much struggle. When we plough into the past with the "experiential" model, there will be a change in our way of being and an enrichment in our interactions with others. The book has a second part dealing with sex abuse in childhood and disruptive relationships.

Bibliography

Al-Khalili and Mc Faddem Johnjoe (2014) Life on the Edge. The coming of age of Quantum Biology. Weidenfeld & Nicolson Ltd. London

Boncinelli Edoardo (2000) The brain, the mind and the soul – Byology. Ed. Mondadori

Bosio Madeline (2018) You shall thank your enemies and love your story.

Bosio Madeline (2018) A psychotherapy?... No... A lifetime

Buber Martin. I and Thou (1987). Collier Books Macmillan Publishing comp. NY

Capra Fritjof. (2000) The Tao of Physics. Amazon

Christine A. Courtois, Ph, D. (1988). Healing the incest wound: W.W. Norton & Company: New York

Dale Peter (1999) Adults Abused As Children: Sage Publications London

Dalai Lama. (2012) Beyond Religion: Hasper Collins. India New Delhi

Faber B.-Brink D. Ruskin P. (1996) The Psychotherapy of Carl Rogers.The Guilford Press.

Gendlin E. (1981) Focusing: New York Banton Books.

Gendlin E. (1984) "The client's client: the edge of awareness" in R. Levant & J

Hawking Stephen (1996) A Brief History of Time. Bantam Books. New York, New York

Shlien: The Client-Centred therapy and the Person-Centred approach: New York Praeger.

Levine Peter A. Ph.D – Maggie Kline (2007) Trauma through a Child's Eyes: North Atlantic Books.

Levine Peter A.Ph.D. In An Unspoken Voice. How the body releases trauma and restores goodness: North Atlantic Books- California.

Maslow Abraham H. (1962) Toward A Psychology Of Being: D. Van Nostrand Company. Inc. New York.

Meluzzi Alessandro (1986) Scatole Cinesi . Dedicato a Gregory Bateson. Mensile : Secondo Natura Maggio 1986.

Mukherjee S. (2016) The Gene –Penguin Random House, India

Nerburn Kent,Ph.D – Louise Mengelhoch, M.A (1991) Native American Wisdom: New World Library – Novato-Canada.

Porges Stephen W. (2011) The Polyvagal Theory: Neurophysiological Foundations Of Emotions, Attachment, Communications and Self-regulation: Norton

Rogers Carl (   ) On Becoming A Person: Houghton Miffin Company – Boston

Rogers Carl (1980) A Way Of Being: Miffin Company-Boston Ma

Salter Anna C. (1995) Transforming Trauma. A guide to understanding and treating adult survivors of child sexual abuse: Sage Publications – London.

Siegel Daniel (2012) The Developing Mind. The Guilford Press. Division of Guilford Publications Inc.

Spinelli Ernesto (1989) The Interpreted World. An introduction to Phenomenological Psychology. Sage Publications London. New Delhi